ABC'S OF FINCHES
KW-151

Contents

Photography: Joshua Charap and Herschel Frey, 49 (top), 63 (bottom), 75 (top). Michael Gilroy, front and back endpapers, title page, 7, 9, 11, 13, 15, 17, 19, 25, 27, 29, 31, 33, 35, 37, 39, 41, 47, 51, 55, 57, 59, 63 (top), 71, 79, 83, 87, 91 (top). Harry V. Lacey, 21, 23, 43. Dan Martin, 49 (bottom), 61, 91 (bottom). Mervin F. Roberts, 67, 75 (bottom). W. A. Starika, 48, 53. Photo on page 45 courtesy of Midori Shobo, Japan.

Drawings by John R. Quinn.

Distributed in the UNITED STATES by T.F.H. Publications, Inc., One T.F.H. Plaza, Neptune City, NJ 07753; in CANADA to the Pet Trade by H & L Pet Supplies Inc., 27 Kingston Crescent, Kitchener, Ontario N2B 2T6; Rolf C. Hagen Ltd., 3225 Sartelon Street, Montreal 382 Quebec; in CANADA to the Book Trade by Macmillan of Canada (A Division of Canada Publishing Corporation), 164 Commander Boulevard, Agincourt, Ontario M1S 3C7; in ENGLAND by T.F.H. Publications Limited, Cliveden House/Priors Way/Bray, Maidenhead, Berkshire SL6 2HP, England; in AUSTRALIA AND THE SOUTH PACIFIC by T.F.H. (Australia) Pty. Ltd., Box 149, Brookvale 2100 N.S.W., Australia; in NEW ZEALAND by Ross Haines & Son, Ltd., 18 Monmouth Street, Grey Lynn, Auckland 2, New Zealand; in the PHILIPPINES by Bio-Research, 5 Lippay Street, San Lorenzo Village, Makati Rizal; in SOUTH AFRICA by Multipet Pty. Ltd., 30 Turners Avenue, Durban 4001. Published by T.F.H. Publications, Inc. Manufactured in the United States of America by T.F.H. Publications, Inc.

THE ABC'S OF
FINCHES

Terry Dunham

Selecting

Star Finch, male.

Did you just buy your first finch? Or have you been keeping and breeding finches for years? In either instance, this book should prove useful to you. It was written for both the novice and the experienced aviculturist—a task not as difficult as one might imagine.

Beginners have many questions: What birds should I buy? How should I care for them? Can I breed them? Will they sing? How long will they live? A handful of questions cascades into seeming hundreds. Each day, a few are answered— and a few new ones arise.

In just the same way, new questions keep occurring to those of us who have been keeping birds for years and raising some of the most challenging species with considerable success. Each "solution" seems to lead to a new question. Perhaps that's why this hobby is so appealing. For beginner and bona fide breeder alike, there is always something new to learn.

I've learned *something* useful from every bird book I've read, no matter how incomplete or out-of-date it seemed to be. And I've picked up something of use from every breeder I've talked to, no matter how ill-advised I may have considered some of his or her methods.

My objective in the pages that follow is to anticipate your questions and to give practical answers to as many of them as possible. Many of these questions will be ones I've asked over the years; others are questions that remain—unanswered—on my mind today. You may discover the answers to some of them. If you do, I hope you will share the answers with me and other aviculturists in the pages of one of the several helpful magazines listed later in this book. Your money will be well spent if you subscribe to these publications— you'll find yourself awaiting their arrival as eagerly as new eggs under your most prized pair of birds!

Why Finches?

Birds can bring the out-of-doors into your home, just as plants do, but even more dramatically. That's reason enough for many people. One or more finches in a cage, even if you never breed them, can add life to a home through color,

– Selecting

White-headed Nun *(Lonchura maja)*, adult.

sound, and activity.

They're not as loud as dogs, not as bossy as cats, and not as sensitive as fish. Every kind of pet has its own virtues, of course, but for many people finches can be the ideal pets. Even so, there are decisions to be made: Should you buy one, or a pair—and how do you tell if two birds *are* a pair? Some pairs of finches will fight, and others will not—what are the behavioral characteristics of the species you're considering? Maybe you'd rather mix species, like colors on an artist's palette— but which ones are compatible? Obviously, even the simple purchase of a few caged pets requires some further knowledge.

There is an added thrill that comes with breeding your pets, a thrill I believe emerges from deep within our psyche and is then compounded by the modern interest in conservation. First, there is anticipation, when what you hope is a pair begins to court, confirming your suspicions. This is followed, if all goes well, by nest building. Dozens of things can go wrong, but eventually the first egg is laid, and then the eggs hatch. The thrill of that success never seems to subside entirely.

I believe a third reason for keeping finches is profit—or, at least, the prospect of profit. Changes in the way birds are brought into this country have radically altered the cost of birds, as you may have noticed when you set out to buy your first pets. Birds cost more today because the government has set up quarantine procedures which must be followed in order to import birds. The quarantine is necessary, the government says, to protect the country's poultry flocks from a destructive viral disease called Exotic Newcastle Disease. Outbreaks of it can cause millions of dollars in losses to poultry farmers; it has happened already. The government's solution is to require all birds entering the country to be quarantined for at least thirty days, during which they are examined and tested. Birds that die are subjected to rigorous autopsies to determine the cause of death. The result, it is hoped, is that birds released from quarantine are not carrying Newcastle Disease. For the most part, the system has worked.

That's the good news. The bad news is that it is extremely costly to operate the kind of quarantine

Fawn-and-White Society
Finch.

station required. The several dozen commercial operations with elaborately designed stations find that their costs have skyrocketed from prequarantine days.

The only alternative is to import your own birds through a government-operated station (there are several). This is no task for the novice, because it involves locating sources of birds overseas and completing a great deal of paperwork and planning beforehand, plus considerable cost as well. You can expect to pay $500 to $1,000 to a customs broker, plus about 30 cents per day per finch during the quarantine period, or about $9 per bird—*plus* each bird's share of the cost of the freight from overseas and the freight to forward the birds to you from the station. And if birds die in quarantine, it's *your* loss! As a result, finches that cost as little as a dollar before the quarantine system can now cost $10 or more just to cover the expense of getting them into the country— and this doesn't include their purchase price overseas.

Birds imported through a commercial station can cost less, but the fact remains that the cost of bringing birds into this country has increased dramatically. This, in turn, has produced a greater demand for birds bred in this country. Hence, economic return has become a third reason why more and more people are keeping birds today.

But there are many kinds of birds. To return to the question prefacing this section, Why finches? There are numerous reasons:

They're cheaper. The cheapest finch costs a little less than the cheapest Budgie. Because finches are smaller, they require less food and smaller—and therefore, cheaper—cages.

They're easier to keep. Because they require less cage space, they're more practical for apartments and homes. Because they're quieter than parrots and parakeets they're easier to live with.

Finally, because smaller birds generally have shorter lifespans and mature more quickly, they also reproduce at an earlier age. Their eggs hatch after fewer days of incubation, and the young are independent at an earlier age. This means they offer, to breeders, major advantages over

Lavender Waxbills *(Estrilda caerulescens).*

larger birds: In three years a finch breeder can be working with his or her third or fourth or even fifth generation of birds. In that same time someone hoping to breed ringnecked parakeets might just be getting the chance to set his or her birds up for breeding for the first time. For aviculturists who exhibit their birds in shows, where they compete for awards based on color and size and other physical characteristics, improved qualities can be "bred into" one's stock in a shorter period of time than is possible with larger birds. New color varieties can be reproduced and established more quickly. For breeders interested in a return on their investment, there is the chance of earlier recovery of at least part of the birds' cost.

Before you misunderstand me about the potential of profiting from your finches, however, be forewarned: many breeders are trying to achieve that objective; only a notable minority succeed at it. There are a multitude of problems that can beset you, as there are in any business. Even success may force you to make choices based on economics rather than personal preference.

Don't let your priorities get misplaced.

If you've ever enjoyed a Goldfinch at your backyard bird feeder or a House Finch in your eaves, you've enjoyed a finch. Some of our native birds—the Cardinal, for example—are kept by aviculturists in other countries. But it is not legal in the United States to keep any native bird as a pet without a special and difficult-to-obtain permit. Here our choices are limited to finches from other continents. Australian and African finches are especially popular, for reasons explained in the sections on these birds later in this text. Included among the "exotic finches" available in this country are many species, with various colors and shapes and a variety of songs and personalities. It is important to remember, when you get your finches and consider the best ways of caring for them, that just as they are alike in many ways, so are they also different, species- by-species and bird-by-bird. One of the most important differences, we will see, depends on whether the birds were trapped in the wild and imported into this country, or bred in captivity (here or

Fawn Zebra Finch, a male.

abroad) and then offered for sale.

Will You Do Well With Finches?

Yes, if you use common sense. People with "green thumbs" do well with plants because they observe events in their gardens or indoor pots and react intelligently to them. You can bring the same simple logic to your efforts with birds, and with good results.

But you *will not* do well if you believe there is only one right way to do things; you will not do well if you refuse to weigh alternative opinions. Don't believe *all* of what anyone tells you, including me. Trust someone who tells you, "This worked for me, so it might work for you." Have healthy skepticism for anyone who says, "You can't do it that way," or "That won't work," or "You must do it this way." They're making the mistake of generalizing their own experiences into a natural law.

You *will* do well with finches if you care about them and demonstrate that care by seeking information wherever you can find it. Your pet store, local breeders, your library—all can and should be resources for you to rely on.

You *will not* do well if you buy species inappropriate for your conditions or if you create conditions inappropriate for your birds.

Buying Finches.

It would be nice if you were reading this section prior to buying your first finches. Unfortunately, too many of us buy *Consumers' Reports* to read about the product we've just brought home, rather than studying it prior to going shopping! Don't skip this section, however, even if your first finches are now happily flitting about in their cage in your living room. You'll probably find they bring you a great deal of pleasure, and you'll buy many more in years to come. The tips in this section are designed to help you with the selection process, whether you've bought one finch or dozens; they may help you avoid disappointment or to make a wiser investment.

"Guarantees" will vary from seller to seller. Be absolutely

Red-cheeked Cordonbleu
(Uraeginthus bengalus), pair.

certain what the terms of the sale are *before* you close the deal. Don't be too critical or suspicious of the breeder or dealer who won't "make good" on birds you buy and which die. There are many things that can go wrong that the seller has no control over. On the other hand, trust your judgment; if something about a bird looks wrong, don't let the seller convince you you're imagining things. If you follow the suggestions here, you'll be doing all you can to minimize the risks involved in buying birds.

Before you start to evaluate the appearance of the birds you want to buy, size up the overall appearance of the place they're coming from. Cleanliness is a good indication of how the birds are cared for. But don't gauge cleanliness by looking at the floor of the cage: The droppings of healthy birds dry quickly, and birds spend most of their time on perches, not the floor. The floors may be dirty with dried droppings and hulls of seeds, and yet the environment may be a healthy one. Look instead at the cleanliness of the perches, waterers, and feeders. If they are dirty, the birds are not properly cared for, and you'd be wise to

pass up the purchase no matter how good individual birds look. Some people, of course, will find it impossible to resist the opportunity to "save" the birds by giving them a better (cleaner) home. They'll regret it.

If the environment passes this test, then look at the birds themselves. Are they sleek, with smooth plumage, clear eyes, and clean feathers around their vents? That's what a healthy bird looks like. Conversely, birds that are sick or stressed may "fluff up" to maintain their body temperature, just as we wrap in a blanket when we're chilled. Healthy birds typically dart about their cage or at least appear alert; sick birds will be less active. Even a healthy bird may rest on its perch during the day with its head tucked back between its wings. A finch sleeping on the floor of its cage or aviary, on the other hand, should *always* be avoided.

Try to find out whether the birds are wild-caught or captive-bred. Captive-bred specimens are almost always worth a premium price. I'll explain why later.

You should also read about the species of finch you're considering buying, prior to making the purchase. Some may

Selecting

Green Twinspot *(Mandingoa nitidula)*.

require food you simply can't provide; some may thrive only in large aviaries. Some are singers, while others have no song; some are hard to breed, some easy. Some are compatible with other birds their own size, and others are just plain mean. Some go through an "eclipse" plumage: at some times during the year they look nothing like the way they'll look the rest of the time. If you want to get a true pair (male and female), you should read about the ways to tell the sexes of that particular species apart, too. To help you with these considerations, there are sections later in this book describing the various species you're most likely to be able to buy in this country, at this time.

Ask how old the birds are, too. Some breeders will buy only adult birds, old enough to breed, and in "full color" (adult plumage). They reason that this averts the risk of the birds dying during their first molt, which sometimes happens. This approach also permits the birds to be set up for breeding immediately, which appeals to the impatient. And it assures the buyer as to the sexes of the birds, which may not be possible with birds in their immature plumage.

As always, there's another voice to be heard. Some breeders choose to buy immature specimens when possible. I'm in this camp. By buying young birds you never get stuck with an unscrupulous breeder's infertile or very old specimens. More importantly, you get to acclimate the birds to your own conditions before you set them up to breed. When they're used to your conditions, they're much more likely to go to nest. Because finches mature so rapidly, buying young stock delays your breeding program only very slightly.

In Review: Make sure you're selecting species you can care for properly. Decide whether you want wild-caught or captive-bred specimens. Review the conditions in which they've been kept, and then the appearance of the birds themselves. Establish the terms of the guarantee, if any, and get it in writing if possible. Finally, make your purchase only *after* having made preparations to acclimate the birds in their new home, as outlined in the following section.

Selecting

Shafttail Finches, once acclimated, prove to be hardy.

Acclimating New Birds.

Don't make the mistake of getting so excited about a beautiful and lively finch that you buy it before you've made arrangements for keeping it. You should consider where in your home you'll keep the bird and what you'll keep it in. That means—at a minimum—buying the proper cage, feeder and waterer, and seed. You can spend a lot or a little for a cage, or you can make your own. In any case, the tips in the following chapter may help you avoid some annoying mistakes that can be made in selecting a cage and the equipment to go with it.

I'm entirely convinced that most of the disappointment that comes when a new bird dies after being taken home can be avoided if only the new owner will follow a few simple rules. Often it's the individual who already owns birds who's most likely to suffer losses because he or she has overlooked these principles.

The philosophy is simple enough: Stress is a tremendous peril for high-strung finches; avoid stress, and you'll avoid a high percentage of losses that would otherwise occur. How do you prevent your birds from being stressed?—like this:

1. Put them into a clean cage. If other birds have been in it before them, clean it thoroughly. This means scrubbing it with a disinfectant and allowing it to dry in the sun. Perches too should be cleaned with the same care, or replaced.

2. Give them the same sort of diet they've been getting. Change diets on a human suddenly, and you're likely to end up with a sick human. The same is true of birds. That's why it's so important to determine how the birds have been kept before you take them home. Once they start looking distressed, often it's too late to alter their environment and save them.

3. Remember to use the same kinds of feeders and waterers they're used to. Some birds will starve before they discover they can reach food by sticking their heads through the bars of their cage to a feeder fastened on the outside; some may die of thirst, if they've been used to drinking from bowls of water, before they discover there's water in a tiny spout at the bottom of a tube or bottle. Take nothing for granted.

4. *Never* take new birds home

Tricolored Nuns *(Lonchura malacca malacca)*.

and put them in with your other birds. No matter how inconvenient it may be, put them in a clean cage, in a different room, separate from the rest of your birds. Keep them there for several weeks, making sure they have adjusted to the initial move without being stressed, before you subject them to the additional stress of joining another group of birds harboring their own bacteria, colds, or other minor afflictions. The birds you buy may be entirely healthy; so may be your own birds. Mixing the two can nevertheless be disastrous. Acclimating the new birds first gets them over the initial stress of moving. They're then better prepared to resist whatever they'll encounter when you add them to your collection. I believe this is the most valuable lesson any bird fancier can learn. I see it ignored over and over again. That's one reason why, when we sell birds we've raised, their new owners are told: "When the birds go out of our door, the deal is final."

As you might imagine, there are other sources of stress: Children with urges to poke through the bars of the cage are not compatible with finches.

Dogs, cats, or a parrot perching on top of the finch cage and screaming will also have a deleterious affect. Also, birds that have been given flight in large aviaries will be stressed if they are moved into small cages. Having said all of this, it is also true that today many finches are domesticated or are approaching it. Once they are *used* to their new owner and new home, they will readily become accustomed to considerable "interference," even during the breeding season. I have Gouldian Finch hens that sit on their eggs so tightly that I must lift them off in order to inspect the nest or to candle the eggs for fertility. Because these birds are *used* to my fingers poking in their nests, they quickly return to the eggs after I'm through. You will reach that stage only gradually with your birds. Start with what *they* are used to. Take your time to get them used to new conditions. You and the birds will be much happier for it.

Care

African Silverbill (*Lonchura cantans).*

The only reason buying a bird cage can be confusing is that there are so many to choose from. Nevertheless, there are only a few variables you need be concerned with:
1. Is it big enough for the bird or birds you want to keep in it?
2. Is it easy enough to clean or to keep clean?
3. Will it accommodate the accessories (feeders, nests, etc.) you want to use in it?
Other considerations, such as price and attractiveness, are of concern to you, too. But you'll have to resolve these issues for yourself. If attractiveness doesn't matter, but price is of extreme importance, you might choose to build your own cages. There's a section in this chapter on how best to do that.

What size cage do you need? In many pet stores you can see a fairly large parrot in a fairly small cage. A finch cage in the same relative proportion might be the size of an old-fashioned box camera—but it would be entirely too small for a finch, which has an entirely different personality from a parrot. Finches are very active birds. They'll fly from perch to perch, or leap from one side of the cage to the other.

Some species are calmer than others. But they all like a little room, certainly more room than the parrot in the preceding example.

A simple rule of thumb might be that finches need a minimum of a cubic foot of cage space per bird—that's a space 12 x 12 x 12 in. This means that a minimum-sized cage for a pair of finches would be about 18 x 18 x 18 in. By this standard, most of the modest-sized cages you'll find in a pet store can perhaps accommodate one pair of finches. There are larger, display-type cages that can either hold more birds or give a single pair the extra room they might need or prefer. But, as a general rule, the standard commercial cages are not big enough to keep two pairs of breeding birds together.

Consider also that a cage of this size is extremely confining for birds that have until recently been flying free, unrestrained, in the wild. You'd be far wiser to buy captive-bred birds if you plan to keep them in a cage of this size. It would even be preferable to get birds that had been raised in cages, as opposed to ones that were raised in aviaries, since the latter too will

24

The Blue-faced Parrot-Finch
(*Erythrura trichroa*) is green on
the throat and breast.

be used to having more room than this comparatively small cage provides. A number of the domesticated species can breed in cages this size: Society Finches, Owl Finches, and Star Finches, for example. But remember that serious bird breeders, intent on maximizing production and protecting the health and strength of their breeding stock, seldom keep valuable breeding pairs in cages this small.

There are larger cages available, sometimes at considerable cost, ranging from small "flight cages" to mini-aviaries on wheels, with enough room for several breeding pairs, or for a dozen finches of various species if breeding is not a primary concern. These can be handsome pieces of furniture that contribute to dramatic interior decorating. Your best bet, if you're planning to breed your new pair of finches, is to buy as large a cage as you can.

How easy will it be to keep the cage clean? Some cages are a lot easier to clean than others. Check to see how the tray or bottom can be removed for cleaning. Does the tray slide out, leaving yet another bottom in place, so the birds cannot escape? Do the sides drop straight down to the bottom, or do they slope in at the bottom? If they slope inward, the droppings from birds resting at the ends of the perches will build up on those sloping sides, rather than fall to the cage floor, where they can be removed.

Also look at the cage and ask yourself this: is there room to position the perches so that none of the feeders are beneath them or within several inches to either side of them? You want droppings to fall directly to the floor, not on feeders, other perches, or other items you're trying to keep clean. Plastic cage bottoms are nice because you can hose them out, soak them in disinfectant, or otherwise clean them thoroughly.

There's another important aspect of cleanliness to consider: how hard is it going to be to keep the area around this cage clean? Even small birds can make quite a mess when they flap their wings and scatter seed hulls into the air. The bamboo cages often sold at import shops are probably the handsomest—and most inconvenient—cages made today. They have only a quarter-inch-high lip around the bottom, if they have any lip at all. Every

Care

Purple Grenadier *(Uraeginthus ianthinogaster),* male.

seed hull in the cage is eventually knocked out onto the floor beneath the cage. If you don't mind vacuuming every day, this won't bother you. For most of us, it's an incredible inconvenience. There are some well-designed cages on the market today with three- to five-inch-high plastic bottoms, which confine most of the seed hulls to the cage itself.

Will the accessories fit in the cage? Remember the fella who built a boat (or airplane, or whatever legend is reported in your area) in his basement (or garage or living room) and then discovered he couldn't get it out? He had the option of chopping off the mast (or wings) to resolve his problem.

If you're not careful, you could end up with a cage you can't get a nest into. It's happened before. So make sure the doors are big enough to accommodate the size of nest you will need to use, or the size of feeder. A big door can be a disadvantage because small birds make a habit of darting past your hand when you reach in to service the cage. But it's better to have a big door and to fashion a second cover for it, with a smaller hole just the size of your hand,

than it is to get a cage you can't use the way you had planned because the door is not big enough.

Building Your Own Cages.

Some people build their own cages to save money. Others do it because they want even bigger or fancier cages than are on the market. Let's look at these alternatives one at a time.

The cheapest way to build a cage is to buy hardware cloth, bend it into the shape and size you want, and fasten the loose ends with C-clips. C-clips can hold doors on—a clothespin functions as a lock—and the result is a cage that is absolutely as functional as any commercial cage, for a fraction of the cost—and with a fraction of the attractiveness. You can design these cages so that the bottom is an inch off the floor, for example. Droppings then fall through onto newspaper beneath, which is periodically changed. For large batteries of breeding cages, this method can be very useful.

Large cages can be built using this same method, but they will require some wooden framework

28

Care

for structural strength. The section on aviaries gives more details on making these. As you get more experienced at cage construction, you may choose to add spring-loaded doors, feeders that fasten to the outside, nests that fasten to doors that swivel open for nest inspection, or whatever other practical innovations you come up with.

The other usual home-made cage is the box-cage, with solid floor, back, sides, and top, usually made of wood. A single piece of hardware cloth is fastened to the front. These cages give the birds kept in them greater privacy, but less light; and, since they're heavier, they're a little more difficult to work with. Some dealers sell cage fronts, which are manufactured wire fronts that are more attractive than what you can make yourself. Some have very nice sliding doors that close automatically—like spring-loaded doors, a great boon should you ever forget to close them.

Half-inch by half-inch hardware cloth is probably the easiest to work with, and may be cheaper than other sizes. Half-inch by one-inch wire mesh has fewer bars, so the birds can more

easily be seen in a cage made of it. Half-inch by three-inch wire is useful, but it's not always available.

Quarter-inch plywood is useful too for box cages. Try to get what's called "marine" plywood, which is treated to resist moisture and will last longer. You'll need to use heavier wood for the bottom, so there's something to fasten the thin plywood to; putting a framework of quarter-rounds in the corners will accomplish the same goal. Very efficient sheet-metal trays can be custom-made at modest cost. Tinsmiths have machines that can make the precise bends in the metal necessary for the trays to fit tightly into the cages. Check your Yellow Pages.

Larger "cages" that are really indoor aviaries can be built using the methods described in the section on aviaries. For very attractive indoor cages and flights you are limited really only by your imagination and carpentry skills. I've seen outstanding examples with built-in, indirect lighting, live plants, and woodwork rivalling the nicest furniture. Just remember that every material you use in the cage's construction might be

Care

Gouldian Finches, male and female.

nibbled on by your pets; make sure you're using safe materials.

Aviaries.

Aviaries can be as much a part of your landscaping as the most exotic plant—and even more satisfying, because of the rich colors, movement, and song live finches can bring to the garden. They can also be a disappointment when they're not well planned.

There are parts of the country where outdoor aviaries are impractical for finches. You may live in Michigan and have wild finches visiting your bird feeder even when it's below zero and there's a foot of snow on the ground. The exotic finches you'll find for sale will never thrive in this kind of weather. They're from warm parts of Africa and Australia, for the most part, and even though domesticated ones now do quite well in temperatures far cooler than their wild ancestors ever experienced, they should not be considered for wintering outdoors.

The ideal aviary partially overcomes this concern, for part of it is indoors. The outdoor section is connected to a building or a room of a house, with a small opening so that the birds can come inside when it's cold, and go outside when it's not. If it were only that simple, all would be trouble-free—it's not. Despite your best efforts to get your birds to breed and feed in the indoor portion during the winter, and to fly outside for exercise and sun, your effort is probably doomed to failure. Your best pair will start building a nest in the outdoor portion just as the worst winter storm heads your way! You're probably better off leaving aviaries to those in warm climates.

Are you sure you want an aviary? If you live in an area with cats running loose (or opossums, raccoons, or other wild animals), you may end up worrying about your birds more than you enjoy them. Sometimes these obstacles may be insurmountable. If you live in California or Florida or any other warm part of the South, add snakes to the list of wild animals you must be concerned about, because there's hardly a way to build an aviary that can be wholly secure from snakes. But if you've got a dog to stand guard against all sorts of

The Green Singing Finch
(Yellow-fronted Canary,
Serinus mozambicus) belongs
to the family Fringillidae.

predators, including snakes and thieves, then you can proceed to the planning stage.

Select a location that is both sheltered and still receives some sun each day. Aviaries can be free-standing in the center of your yard if you include some sheltered areas in them. But the most practical location is often in a corner of your yard where fences or angles of your home enclose two sides, leaving the others open for ventilation, rain, and sun.

Aviaries need to have at least part of their roofs covered. You can cover them with marine-grade plywood. You can put that roof on a slant and shingle it if you want to. You can also cover the roof, or part of it, with corrugated fiberglass, which allows some light in but keeps rain out. You still want to have part of the roof open. On the most miserable of days, you'll find your birds happily dancing beneath the leaking spot in the roof, if you've covered it all, bathing themselves and preening afterwards. In all likelihood they'll be healthier for this exposure. Drafts are the biggest danger; even exotic finches can survive freezing temperatures

occasionally, *if* they're used to them. But the combination of cold, wind, and dampness can prove fatal for any of them.

Live plants enhance an aviary, give the birds nesting sites, and add to the birds' general security. You might consider plantings immediately outside the aviary too—not so that they block all your view, but so that some ends or corners are well hidden. The birds will probably nest in these areas.

There are numerous ways to build aviaries. One of the easiest I've found is with hardware cloth and 2 x 2 pine. Cut the 2 x 2s to the desired length and drill through the crosspieces you'll be nailing through into the ends of other 2 x 2s. Use good-sized nails; because you've predrilled the holes with slightly smaller drill bits, you won't split the wood, and you can drive the nails directly into the ends of the connecting pieces. The resulting frame will be very wobbly, but you can square it up, using a carpenter's square, as you staple the hardware cloth to the frame. The wire will give the aviary the rigidity it needs. One of the most convenient tools I've found for making aviaries, by the way, is

Red-headed Gouldians are the
most common in captivity.

the electric staple gun. You'll be
surprised how many staples you'll
drive in the course of building an
aviary of substantial size, and the
cramps and pain in your hand
from the use of a conventional
stapler can be equally substantial.

Creosote sealant will protect
even cheap pine from rotting and
bugs for years. It is a powerful
skin irritant, so you should wear
clothes that cover all of your
body, as well as plastic goggles,
when you use it. Once it's soaked
into the wood, I've never
observed a harmful effect from it
on the birds.

Many books advise you to dig
a trench around your aviary and
extend the wiring 18 in. into the
earth. I've never done that; my
aviaries rest on the surface of the
ground, and though mice and
snakes can get into them, they
don't need to dig in order to do
so, because they can squeeze
through small slots between
doors, etc.

Don't forget to add a safety
walk, which is a small enclosure
you walk into before entering the
aviary itself. This protects against
birds flying past you to their
freedom when you enter. You
might also want to add small
doors so that the aviary can be

serviced from outside. This way,
you don't disturb the birds at
feeding time. The greater sense
of security will give wild-caught
stock more confidence for going
to nest.

Don't get the idea that the
bigger the aviary, the more
breeding results you'll have,
because that's simply not the case
unless you're dealing with a very
shy and easily spooked species
direct from the wild. Given 100
sq. ft. of aviary space, there is no
question that ten pairs of birds
will produce more babies in 10
separate 10 sq. ft. flights than
they will if they're all turned
loose into the single large space.
Even those species that are
colony breeders in the wild will
be stimulated by their proximity
to others of their kind, but the
absence of interference will do
wonders for their procreative
urges. I'm firmly convinced, in
fact, that some birds breed more
rapidly in cages, simply because
there is nothing to do but eat and
breed, whereas in a large planted
aviary there are dozens of
distractions.

One safety feature you won't
want to overlook is a low-
wattage night-light. Many birds
die in aviaries simply because

Diamond Sparrow (Diamond Firetail, *Emblema guttata*).

they're startled—by a predator or a backfiring car or whatever. Darting from their nest or perch and unable to see in the dim light, they crash into the wire at the far end of the aviary. Let the birds have just enough light to be able to see where they're going.

Finally, there's one other nice feature about an aviary: it requires less maintenance effort. Look at it this way: Ten pairs of birds in ten cages require ten feeders and waterers, which must be cleaned and filled. Ten cages must be cleaned. In an aviary, those same birds require one-tenth the feeders and waterers. Because their droppings fall on soil and can be periodically scraped up or hosed down or simply taken care of by nature, if the aviary's not overcrowded, cage cleaning may be a thing of the past. Each aviculturist must weigh breeding results against the time available for caring for the collection, and choose the balance of cages and aviaries he or she wants.

Providing a healthy diet for your finches is a relatively simple task. They must have clean seed and clean water to survive—that's all. The rest of the dietary items mentioned here are supplements. There's a big difference, of course, between a bird that's *surviving* and a bird that's *thriving*, and much of that difference will be the result of periodically offering as many as possible of the supplements your birds will eat.

The Seed Mix.

Finches eat various kinds of plant seeds. Among those most commonly available from pet stores and feed stores are canary seed, millet, oats, and thistle (niger). If canary and millet seeds are mixed together, the result is called finch mix, but the exact proportion of those seeds will vary depending upon who you buy your seed from. Some suppliers carry "fancy finch" mixes that may include oats or thistle or both, plus other seeds and more than one kind of millet.

Since a varied diet is to the birds' advantage, you should try to find a good mixture. It will

Feeding

Green Twinspot (*Mandingoa nitidula*).

even look prettier than plain finch mix because it will include more differently colored and shaped seeds. Your birds may have a marked preference for just one of the kinds of seeds in the mix, however. If this is the case, they may knock all the mix from the feeder in an effort to feed solely on their favorite seed. You may or may not be able to break them of this habit. Also, some species prefer certain kinds of seeds to others. Owl Finches will eat a greater proportion of small millet; Goulds will often show a preference for canary seed and large white millet; The Black-hooded Red Siskin will eat large portions of thistle and prefers canary seed to finch mix. Be sure to read all you can about the species of finches you're going to keep, to understand their particular seed preferences.

Once you know what kinds of seeds your birds need, you'll need to know what those seeds look like, so you can evaluate the mixes you have to choose from.

Canary seed is light brown in color, relatively flat, rather than round, and has points at both ends.

Millet is a round seed. There are many different kinds, ranging from very small to rather large, and from yellow to brown to reddish-brown in color. Your birds will find spray millet—millet still on the stalk—a special treat and spend much of the day picking seeds from it. I use spray millet to teach newly fledged birds to "crack" (hull) seed on their own, since their curiosity and the behavior of older birds in the cage or aviary invariably leads them to pick at it.

Oats are considerably larger seeds; you may recognize them from breakfast cereals. They're often sold "hulled"—with the hull removed, leaving just the kernel, for the birds to eat.

Thistle (niger) is shaped something like canary seed but is black. It's an oily seed, good for birds' plumage and, some breeders believe, for hens about to lay.

Rape is a small, dark brown or black seed. It's added to some "deluxe" canary mixes.

There are numerous other seeds you can buy separately or find in some mixes, ranging from extremely fine grass seeds to celery seeds to hemp, which is in the marijuana family and therefore is sold only after being irradiated so it cannot germinate.

Feeding

All these seeds are good for the birds that count on you for their care. If you also keep larger birds, occasionally dump the chewed kernels left in sunflower-seed feeders into your finch aviary or cage; the finches will eagerly pick through the hulls for bits of sunflower and will benefit from the added variety in their diet.

If you're especially interested in the seeds you're feeding your birds, turn to one of the books that deals at greater length with bird nutrition. Scientists have analyzed the nutritive contents of the various seeds, and you may enjoy speculating on why your birds eat more of one than another in warmer or colder seasons, for example, or when they have babies.

Sprouted Seed.

Sprouted seed is especially good for your birds because just when seed begins to germinate (grow) it contains more nutrients than when it is still dry. There are a multitude of methods of sprouting seed; rather than try one of the esoteric approaches, use this simple method:

1. Go to a health-food store and buy a seed sprouter. Make sure you get one in which the screen is small enough so that your bird seed will not pass through.

2. Fill the jar about one-third full of seed, add water, shake it vigorously, and pour off the water. Repeat. Fill the jar and allow the seed to soak. Do this in the morning.

3. That evening pour off the water. Refill the jar, shake it, and again pour off the water, then refill again. Allow to soak overnight.

4. The next morning, rinse several times, as you have done before. Pour off the water. Place the jar on its side so that air can pass through to the seed. Allow it to sit this way all day. That evening (thirty- six hours after the process began) rinse the seed again several times, pour off the water, and again place the jar on its side.

5. The next morning you should find tiny white shoots just beginning to grow from most of the seeds. Rinse thoroughly, pour off the water, and feed. It may take your birds a few days to get used to it, but they will. And when they do, they'll be getting additional nutrition.

42

Chestnut-breasted Mannikin
(Lonchura castaneothorax).

Greens, Water, and Grit.

In the wild, finches routinely pick at the leaves of plants. Green food is an important part of their natural diet. You should see that once or even several times a week they get a small bit of leafy vegetable. Check the produce section of your supermarket, again seeking occasional variety: carrot tops, kale, spinach, and other darker green vegetables are good. Iceberg lettuce contains a high percentage of water and may not be quite as good for your birds as these other greens. Shredded carrots will be appreciated too and will enhance the natural colors of some species.

Clean water is vital for your birds' health. One of the easiest ways to add vitamins to your birds' diet is in their drinking water. You may need to add them slowly, however, for some have a distinctive taste, and the birds may not drink the water until they've gotten used to the taste. Watch—and use your head.

At one time I believed grit was not necessary for birds' health. I now believe it is. You can get grit at almost any pet store. Offer it in a small cup in the cage, where the birds can get it when they want or need it. On rare occasions birds may overindulge in it, if they've been without it for a long time, so you may want to sprinkle just a tiny amount on the cage floor at first, then slowly add more until you have it always in front of your birds. When I add a new cup of grit to my cages of Gouldian Finches, some of them head directly to it, even before eating any of the greens or soft food added at the same time.

Live Foods and Egg Food.

Mealworms are the most practical live food. You can get them from your pet store, or you can order them by mail from suppliers who advertise in various bird publications, or you can even raise your own. They are not essential to your birds' health, but, as explained in some of the sections on the various species of finches, they may stimulate breeding, particularly in birds that were trapped in the wild and still have strong instinctive needs.

If you want to experiment with other live foods, you can raise maggots (yes, you read that

Feeding

right!) or fruit flies. I found a correlation between offering termites to my Violet- eared Waxbills and their going to nest, but this may not be sufficient reason to duplicate that experiment.

The best substitute for live food is egg food, since both are high in protein. There are about as many different recipes for egg food as there are breeders. Ask your pet-store owner or a local breeder what he or she uses, or try this formula: Hard-boil an egg. Peel it, mash the white and the yolk, and then sprinkle it with soy-protein powder (from a health-food store), wheat-germ flakes, and any brand of powdered vitamin-mineral supplement offered by your pet store. Add enough of the powdered ingredients, stirring them into the mashed egg, so that the resulting egg food is fairly dry and crumbly. Then feed it to your birds. Birds feeding babies will devour it as soon as they're used to it. Be sure to use containers you can wash frequently. Many breeders will tell you that you must remove uneaten egg food an hour or two after it's offered. While it's true bacteria does grow in egg, we

leave ours in the cage until the next morning, and even in humid Florida I have seen no health problems resulting from this practice. If the egg food visibly spoils, of course, it should be removed, and you should add more powder in the future to keep it drier.

There are all sorts of other diet supplements, and virtually any of them that your birds will eat are good for them. However, don't feel that you must offer them more than good seed, clean water, and occasional greens and egg food; birds can happily breed and live long and healthy lives on exactly this regimen.

Top: Painted Finch (*Emblema picta*), pair. **Bottom:** Hand-rearing Melba youngsters.

If you want to breed finches, you can. You may have to endure some failures, and you may have to make some concessions to the breeding effort. But you can succeed. If you have not yet bought your first finches, you can improve the likelihood of future breeding success by buying species that are most likely to reproduce, such as Society Finches, Zebra Finches, and several of the other Australian finches. If African finches have captured your fancy, go the extra mile—that is, pay the extra dollars to get captive-bred specimens.

What follows is a guide for the beginner. Because it instills the basic principles I still apply to the challenge of breeding any new species, it is to be hoped these pointers will be of value to even the most experienced breeder.

Controlling the Variables.

There are two philosophies of bird breeding. The first holds that you should do what you can to obtain a compatible pair, then set them up and leave them alone. If they haven't bred in six months, or in a year, frustration is understandable. But this philosophy holds that the birds are still getting used to one another and to their environment. You should give them more time. Many intelligent breeders adhere basically to this philosophy, and their birds do raise young. This practice, then, at least warrants consideration.

I swear by the other philosophy—call it the philosophy of *controlled meddling*. Those who believe in this approach will change the variables whenever their birds seem to be in breeding condition but don't breed, or whenever everything seems in order but the birds won't come into breeding condition for some reason.

Red-cheeked Cordonbleu chick with its mother.

48

— Breeding

Cutthroat Finch *(Amadina fasciata)*, pair.

This view considers birds as animals that react to various stimuli. Privacy (or security) is certainly one important stimulus. But all of the following variables are also important. The meddler chooses to change some of those variables, even at the expense of the birds' sense of security, until breeding activity occurs. You would be amazed how many times birds that have shown no interest whatsoever in nesting promptly go to nest following a seemingly insignificant change in their environment. Don't misunderstand. The meddler avoids stressing his or her birds; he may cover a corner of a cage where the nest hangs, to give the hen more security; he recognizes the relatively nervous nature of finches and accommodates it. But he does not let birds set idly for months out of fear of disturbing them.

When you weigh these variables, always keep in mind whether your birds are wild-caught or captive-bred specimens. This can make a big difference in the birds' breeding needs and habits. You'll also be better able to weigh the changes you can make with your birds if you know about the conditions they were kept in before you got them, and, if they're captive-bred birds, the conditions in which they were raised.

Housing.

The cage you've got your birds in may be big enough to keep them healthy but not big enough to make them feel secure enough to want to breed. Birds need a certain amount of room for exercising. They also need to be able to retreat a certain distance from anything they perceive as threatening. Imagine how imposing even a "towering four-foot-tall fifth-grader" can seem to finches confined in a small cage. You can get either a larger cage or an aviary, or cover part of the cage to increase the birds' sense of security. You can also place the cage high up, on a shelf or hook, and the birds will feel more secure.

One of the biggest hurdles to birds' breeding in aviaries is the interference of hawks and snakes and cats and squirrels and mice and other wildlife that keep the birds constantly on edge, just as if they were confined in a small cage with people constantly

walking by. Even tree or shrub branches batting against the wire can keep the birds on edge. Not every aviary has to be this way. You can plant shrubs around yours to shelter the birds, but keep the branches trimmed away from the wire itself. You can put a roof over at least part of the aviary, and keep nests, shelters, or perches in that area as well as in open areas where the birds can soak up rain and sun. You can occasionally set mouse traps in the safety walk, where the birds can't get to them. You can try to discourage the other predators, but in practical terms there may be little you can do that is legal or tolerable to keep owls or hawks (since they are protected wildlife) from driving your birds to distraction.

You can consider subdividing your large aviary into smaller flights; this sometimes helps. If you're colony breeding, hang some vertical "baffles"—nothing more than foot-square pieces of wood—between the nesting sites, so that birds using one nest can't see others nearby. Put the nests higher than the perches, so the nests are the highest things in the flight. Place feeders and waterers where they can be serviced

without entering the aviary and disturbing the birds.

Nests.

In cage or aviary, your birds will do best if offered a variety of nests. You might end up using only one kind, but the initial experiment will establish what kind of nests your birds prefer. Also, face them in different directions; place them at different heights. Some species prefer to nest high; others may want to nest on or near the ground.

Give the birds places where they can build natural nests too, as they would in the wild. If you live in the West, tumbleweeds tied or otherwise fastened in the aviary make excellent nest sites. Elsewhere, try fastening dry but sturdy branches to the wire. Or take chicken wire, wrap it around a basketball-sized mound of hay, and hang that in the flight; some species of birds will eagerly burrow into that ball of hay to build their nests.

Vary the size of the openings on nests; the degree of darkness has a great deal to do with a nest's suitability. There are studies with larger birds that indicate the degree of darkness

Normal (wild-colored) Zebra
Finch male.

even stimulates physical changes in both sexes' reproductive organs, bringing them into breeding condition. Don't forget to offer different sizes of nests too.

I've seen birds refuse to go to nest for months, showing absolutely no interest in each other or in the nests available to them, then suddenly and promptly go to nest when a new kind of nesting material was introduced. Among your choices: green grass clippings; dried grass; unravelled yarn, hemp cord, or burlap; white feathers; tree leaves; various kinds of hay; even strips of different kinds of paper. Vary the lengths. Unravel some of the strands so that they're frizzled. Scatter some on the floor of the cage or on the ground in the aviary. Make a small hardware-cloth tray to hang on the side of the cage or aviary, so the birds can tug the nesting materials from it.

Always mold some sort of minimal nest in the bottom of a wicker nest or box nest before hanging it. Some birds will lay in a nest without ever building in it, and if you've lined the nest, there will be some cushioning to prevent the eggs from breaking

or becoming chilled.

Pairs or Groups?

With some species, the presence of numerous individuals stimulates breeding; with others, all this leads to is perpetual defense of territory and fighting. What's worse, some pairs or groups of birds may directly contradict the generalizations you might make about their species. It's the breeder's responsibility to select the right birds for the setup he or she has, and to then watch them carefully to make the adjustments necessary for reasonably peaceful and productive coexistence.

There will be times when you can only find—or only afford—one pair of a species. After your original choice is made, there is little more you can do to influence the compatibility of the pair. If you can choose from a large number of birds, however, try to select the birds that preen each other or, if they're in adjacent flights, that alight on the wire next to each other. If you've been able to obtain several males and females, house them together at least briefly, after banding

— *Breeding*

them with different-colored plastic bands. Then let them pick their own mates. Once you've seen which males are interacting with which females, set them up that way for breeding.

But, having paired up your birds, don't feel you've got to keep them that way forever. If they don't breed after several months, switch mates. If that seems too extreme to you, just separate the two birds for a week or two and then reintroduce them. Sometimes that's all it takes!

Other Variables.

Obviously, finches in the wild breed seasonally. The more recently they have been taken from the wild, the more closely they may adhere to that timetable. As they become more domesticated, however, they behave differently. Particularly when they are kept indoors, with artificial light creating long days at any time of year or the year around, any of the domesticated strains of finches can breed at any time of the year. At Bird Bay Breeders we keep lights in the birdroom on fifteen hours a day and have Gouldians and other finches breeding vigorously in every month of the year, even though the temperature in the unheated bird house might average in the forties at night in January and in the nineties during the day in August.

Literally every element of your bird-keeping regimen is a variable you can experiment with. Change the diet, but slowly. Change the temperature, if you're indoors, and have observed any indication that a change might be productive. Some birds breed quickly after the rainy season starts, so try misting your birds with a fine water spray each day. Use your imagination. Good luck!

Strawberry Finch (Red Avadavat, *Amandava amandava*), pair.

Australian Finches.

With the exception of the Zebra Finch, the Australian finches are not among the cheapest finches available to American aviculturists. They're important, nonetheless, both because of their beauty and because many of them have been bred in captivity for so long that they can be considered to be *domesticated*.

After the Australian government prohibited the export of its native animals early in the 1960s, finches from that country became harder and harder to obtain. Breeders therefore worked more and more diligently and imaginatively at breeding them. The combination of economic incentive and esthetic appeal was irresistible. And the breeders succeeded admirably. Today the captive populations of many of these species has rebounded, and the prices have declined, making them available to more hobbyists. They're not yet as cheap as the most commonly imported African finches, but at least the situation has improved over the past several decades so that it is no longer likely that most of these species would disappear in America, no matter what international barriers to trade might be imposed in the future.

Ironically, it is the African finches which are imported in the greatest numbers that would be most threatened if imports to the U.S. were suddenly banned. I believe much of what we have learned about breeding the Australian finches in captivity can be applied successfully to the African finches as well, because they are similar in so many ways. Many will quarrel with this opinion, but I have seen many of the Australian finches, once considered delicate and exotic, become reliable breeders, common and hardy. Today some aviculturists predict that Crimson Finches, for example, will never prove just as easy to breed; that Painted Finches have special problems at the time of fledging that will keep them from ever being prolific; that even if the rarest firetail finches are someday imported, they will never be domesticated like the other Australian finches. I think these impressions are more in the minds of the beholder than they are a reflection of reality.

What breeders must guard

Species

Yellow-bellied Waxbills
(_Estrilda melanotis quartinia_).

against, on the other hand, is carelessness—the inclination to take any of these species for granted. When a species, or a new color variety, is considered rare, we lavish attention on it. While too much attention can be counterproductive—if it manifests itself in too-frequent inspections of nests or in locating a cage in a too-easily- observed, and thus disturbed, spot—it can also be productive—if the breeder seeks common-sense solutions to observed problems: moving nests if they inspire no breeding activity in their initial location; doubting and double-checking one's initial conclusions regarding the sexes of birds paired up to breed; varying the diet; or otherwise reacting to all that goes on (or does not go on!) in the breeding cage or flight.

Once a species is breeding readily, we may forget the many details we attended to when first we worked with the species. Many of them can be abandoned, and are unnecessary—but perhaps not all. It is not unusual to have several very successful years followed by seasons of declining production, even if we remember to trade some of our young for unrelated others.

Often-times all it takes to boost productivity back to earlier levels is a careful review of the management methods we practiced during the good years.

Despite their cost, then, Australian finches are ideal birds for the beginner. They are colorful, active, hardy, and will pose for their owners all the mysteries and challenges he or she will encounter with scarcer or more difficult finches. The appearance of new color varieties and of rarer species of Australian finches can keep even the most aggressive breeder satisfied with new challenges. At the other extreme, the common Zebra Finch can provide the perfect introduction to Australian finches at a price that is almost negligible—is negligible in fact, when one considers the great likelihood that breeding success will quickly recoup the owner's initial investment.

Zebra Finch (_Poephila guttata_). Zebra Finches are the cheapest and most varied of the Australian finches. They can be the easiest to breed, or the most frustrating. In a colony situation, they reproduce in such numbers that their breeding shortcomings may not be apparent. In cage

breeding, on the other hand, results may be either astoundingly successful or so bad one will wonder how they've ever become so common!

Because they're so cheap, it's economical to replace an unproductive pair or an errant mate. The "failure" doesn't register on us the way it would with an expensive bird. And since there's such a large pool of replacements available, one never goes through the frustration of searching far and wide for an odd hen or replacement male. These facts alone contribute a great deal to the general success the species has had and make it ideal for the beginner.

The most common problem with Zebra Finches is their habit of building layer upon layer of nests. Typically, this is what happens: A pair has laid and begun incubating, when it is struck by the instinctive urge to go to nest again. Responding to Nature's imperatives, the pair builds a new nest on top of the previous clutch of eggs, and lays again. This can happen as many times as the size of the nest and the availability of nesting materials permit. Many eggs are laid, but no young are produced.

The solutions are many and unreliable. The best bet is to remove excess nesting material as soon as the first nest is built. In an aviary, of course, this will simply drive the offending pair to other nests, where, by stealing enough new nesting material to disrupt their own breeding efforts, they'll also interfere with the other birds housed in the aviary and disrupt *their* breeding too.

These habits force the aviculturist to accept the Zebra Finch *on its own terms*, observing problems carefully and seeking common-sense solutions to the problems that arise. Because their diet, housing requirements, breeding behavior, and many other characteristics so closely parallel those of the other Australian finches, the lessons learned will be useful later no matter what species is being kept.

Zebra Finches are sexually dimorphic; that is, males and females look different from one another, in all the color varieties except the White mutation. And even the Whites can usually be sexed by the male's redder beak, if not by his frequent song-and-dance in courting the female.

— Species —

With Zebra Finches and many other kinds of birds, you can prompt a courtship display by isolating a bird for several days or longer and then introducing, or reintroducing, it to a bird you believe to be of the opposite sex. Birds that have not displayed for months, even in a cage with the same female, for example, are often provoked in this way to a demonstration that establishes their sexual identity beyond any doubt.

In the wild, Zebra Finches and many other Australian finches breed in close harmony with the rainy season that produces the seed heads with which young are fed. Biologists theorize they reach sexual maturity very rapidly because one can never predict when the next rainy season will arrive, and the birds must be prepared to take advantage of it if they are to survive. Whatever the reason, Zebra Finches can breed at four or five months of age, even if they have not yet completely molted into color. There are reports of pairs only three months old breeding successfully. Considering that they are almost a month and a half old before they have reached independence from their parents, the period in which

they reach sexual maturity is obviously brief indeed.

Pairs eager to breed may begin laying again before the first nest of babies has flown. In this case, the new eggs are either broken or soiled so that they cannot hatch, or they hatch while the previous babies are still in the nest, so the hatchlings are often trampled to death in the nest. The careful breeder will watch for this and other complications. This problem can be resolved by removing the second clutch of eggs and either discarding them or fostering them to another pair, or by moving them to a second, clean nest placed next to the first nest. Often one parent, typically the male, will stay with the older youngsters, while the other, usually the hen, will turn to the new nest and continue incubating the new eggs in that safer and more productive location.

Owl Finch (*Poephila bichenovii*). Owl Finches are about the size of Zebra Finches. They're cloaked in generally drab shades of gray and brown, yet the overall appearance is pleasing because of the ring surrounding the face (like a Barn-Owl) and because of the contrast between the light and dark parts of the plumage, especially on males. Males seem frosty-white or silver on the face and chest; hens look as though muddy water had been washed over them, then dried, partly blurring their markings.

Owl Finches will eat mealworms, but these are not essential for breeding, much less for the birds' health. It may be advisable, however, to supplement their seed diet with an egg food such as the one suggested earlier. They'll get the protein they need for reproduction from the egg food, and with far greater ease for the breeder.

Owl Finches in my collection have generally chosen to nest in small wicker nests and have shown a preference for fine and light-colored nesting materials such as unwoven hemp or burlap. Incubation time for eggs, as with all the other Australian finches, is thirteen days. My Owl Finches have averaged perhaps 4.5 eggs per clutch, slightly fewer than Gouldians, Shaftails, or Zebra Finches. They are just as willing as these other species to go to nest, however, and just as willing to continue laying repeated clutches if their eggs are removed and fostered to Society Finches. One of the first pairs that ever bred for me laid about fifty eggs in a dozen clutches; I produced about forty babies that single breeding season because I fostered the eggs to Societies. Your Owl Finches should breed in cages or aviaries.

If your "pair" doesn't lay, test the hypothesis that you've sexed them incorrectly. They build *roosting* nests; the fact that two birds have built or even sit in the nest during the day does not confirm that you've put together a true pair. If your "pair" lays, but the eggs are infertile, test the hypothesis that you've put two hens together. You'll find these tests useful with almost any species.

Star Finch (*Noechmia ruficauda*). Star Finches are slightly larger than Zebra Finches and Owl Finches. They can be drab and unimpressive if they're kept in cages away from direct sunlight for extended periods; they're perhaps the only Australian finch that fades in captivity. In outside aviaries, on the other hand, they can be among the most beautiful of all the finches. The male's head glows in glorious crimson, his back gets rich green, and his chest sports a sun-bright daisy yellow.

Species

Society Finch feeding young.

Whether the colors glow because of the sunlight, the rain baths, or the variety of live foods and greens that can be found in an aviary, I don't know. All that matters, I suppose, is that they do achieve such attractive levels.

We got our first Star Finches around 1974, when they were extremely scarce. Six months later they had about forty young and were still producing, with the help of our friends, the Society Finches. I was running up incredible phone bills searching everywhere for unrelated stock to pair my youngsters to. I succeeded, and within several more months the second generation of our Star Finches were happily popping out of nests. I'll always have a soft spot for Star Finches, because I've built my whole collection by pyramiding the results of that first successful breeding experience. And if I had an outdoor aviary today (we're at present breeding only in a specially-built bird house), Star Finches would be the first species I'd want to introduce to it, for their sheer beauty in that environment.

There are Yellow-headed Star Finches now available in the U.S., but they're more of a curiosity than an improvement on the original. Most Star Finches I've worked with have been poor parents, though they produce fertile eggs quite willingly. Some breeders do have prolific Star Finches, and establishing strains of Star Finches that will raise their own young is a challenge worthy of any breeder.

One final note regarding the young: learning to sex your offspring at an early age can make your bird-room operation much more efficient, because you can hold back only what you need for your own purposes and sell the rest, months ahead of what might otherwise be possible. The easiest way to sex Star Finches and other dimorphic species while they are still very young is to find areas on adult hens and males where the plumage differs in color. Use tweezers to pluck a few feathers from those same areas on immature birds. Within several weeks these feathers will begin to grow back, and when they do, the new feathers will show the colors of the adult birds. On Star Finches two convenient places to pluck are on the forehead, midway between the eyes, and on the chin, just beneath the lower beak. If red feathers grow back in either of

these spots, the bird is a male. On hens, the head feathers will grow in green, the chin feathers buff. Study the adults of any species you're working with, and you'll see how this technique can be used to your advantage.

Shafttail Finch (*Poephila acuticaudata*). Shafttail Finches are handsome, animated, and graceful—and can be maddening because some can be so difficult to sex. Most males have wider bibs (throat patches) than most hens, but sometimes just the opposite is true. Males have an attractive song, but it's not frequently heard. This species breeds fairly readily, so there's little ground for complaint, I suppose. Clutch size averages about five eggs. Like the other Australian finches, Shafttails will lay repeated clutches if their eggs are removed for fostering. And like the other Australian species I've worked with, they're perfectly capable of breeding at six months of age. They'll eat live food but don't have to have it. About half the pairs I've given the chance to rear their own young have done so successfully.

British breeders have produced an all-white Shafttail that is somewhat unrewarding since little would distinguish it from a White Zebra Finch, other than its larger size and longer tail. There's also a pied variety in England; photos I've seen of them are quite attractive. Fawn Shafttails, now available in the U.S., are handsome. They sell for about twice the price of the Normal birds.

Shafttails can and will hybridize with Parson Finches, but there's little to be gained by allowing this. The hybrid offspring are very fertile but not as attractive as either pure species. Shafttails may also hybridize with Masked Grassfinches.

Parson Finch (*Poephila cincta*). The Parson Finch is a stocky version of the Shafttail, with a black beak and a short, squared-off tail. The Parson Finches I've kept had a tendency to get fat if kept in cages. They like mealworms. Though the bib, or throat patch, is usually smaller on hens, that's not always the case. If you see a bird "topping," or copulating with another, don't be fooled into thinking that the second bird is a hen: it's not at all uncommon for males to attempt to top other males.

Masked Grassfinch (*Poephila personata*). Masked Grassfinches are probably the hardest of all the

Australian finches to breed. The difficulty of sexing them probably has a great deal to do with it. Males rarely display, and females frequently build roosting nests that may confuse a breeder into thinking he or she is working with a true pair.

They're pleasant additions to a collection of Australian finches: active, colored differently from most of the other species, and hardy. Their waxy yellow beaks contrast nicely with the colors of many other species, and they're not overly aggressive, as long as you give them sufficent room so that nesting territories are not too close (you should do the same for any other species). Keeping them with others of their genus (Shafttails, Parson Finches), however, runs the risk of unwanted hybrids that are more a nuisance than an asset. They're one of the Australian finches that will relish mealworms, though these are not essential.

Diamond Sparrow (*Emblema guttata*). The Diamond Sparrow is the only one of the Australian firetails available today in America. The others are at best scarce even in Europe, where, if they exist at all, they are probably recently smuggled, wild-caught birds. At worst, the other species are already threatened in their own country, due to destruction of their habitat.

Diamond Sparrows are the largest of the Australian finches. Because they have a tendency to become overweight when kept in cages, their size can be even more impressive, but just as unhealthy. Oats and mealworms should be rationed carefully and the birds kept in as large an enclosure as possible.

Males are most easily identified by behavior and are not reluctant to display that behavior. They'll erect the feathers on the throat and head, crane their heads into the air, and dance up and down on the perch while bobbing and singing. These birds seek out fairly large nests and lay four or five eggs. Though the youngsters are relatively large, good Society Finches will have no difficulty raising four or five if they are fostered. Unlike many of the other Australian finches (Goulds, Stars, Chestnut-breasted Mannikins, and Crimson Finches, for example) which are uniformly colored when they fledge, Diamond Sparrows (like Owl and Shafttail finches, on the other hand) show the adult pattern of colors but in a far paler

Red-cheeked Cordonbleu
(Uraeginthus bengalus),
female.

version. The birds attain adult plumage after their first molt.

Gouldian Finch (*Chloebia gouldiae*). There's no need to describe the adult Gouldian Finch; pictures do that better than words. There are three different head colors, and blue-and white-breasted varieties. Young are drab green above and gray below until they begin their dramatic first molt. Molting usually begins when the birds are about three months old and is complete by the time they're six months old, but there is a great deal of individual variation. In the first molt, the young Gouldian Finch replaces all of its feathers in a few short months. Sometimes half the body seems covered with feather sheaths. Molting can sap the bird's strength and can weaken or kill a youngster.

Nevertheless, Gouldian Finches are not as delicate as earlier literature would have breeders believe. Twenty years ago, some authors estimated that as many as half of all Goulds bred in captivity might die as they struggled through the molt. I don't know anyone who's had misfortune even approaching this level. On the other hand, it is not unusual for five to ten percent of

the youngsters to suffer during this time. They can fluff up and look miserable, until finally the molt is complete and they sleek down and again become active—or they may die.

Water-soluble vitamins will surely help. All the other proper dietary provisions also help the birds stay strong during this sometimes critical stage—grit, greens, fresh seed, clean water, and occasional egg food. There's a poultry product called Ren-O-Sal that can be added to the drinking water. It adds trace arsenic, among other vitamins and minerals, to the birds' intake, and some biologists believe that this strengthens the birds as the molt takes place. Use one-half tablet in a gallon of drinking water.

Gouldians of different head colors will interbreed indiscriminately; a red-head doesn't prefer another red-head to a yellowhead, for example. In the wild, black-headed Goulds outnumber red-heads three to one, and yellow-heads are extremely rare. In captivity breeders have established the yellow-head, so that today all three head colors can be found in significant numbers. Early books stated that yellow-heads were weak; maybe

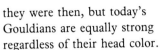

they were then, but today's Gouldians are equally strong regardless of their head color.

There is great disagreement over the temperature requirements of Gouldian Finches. The only valid rule is that you should keep them within the temperature range to which they have become accustomed. "Hot-house" birds kept indoors with thermostatically-controlled minimum temperatures of 72 F. cannot survive if moved outside in midwinter, not even in the South. On the other hand, California breeders whose stock has become hardy over the years may find their Goulds can survive infrequent light snow. In southern California, as in our aviaries in Florida, the birds are occasionally exposed to nights during which the temperature drops below freezing. If the birds are healthy and sheltered from the wind, and if the birds are used to wide-ranging temperatures, they will not suffer.

Temperature is not the only variable you need to concern yourself with if you attempt to keep and breed Gouldian Finches or any of the other Australian finches. You should *be observant* and *ask every question you can* even if you are merely buying

birds from another breeder in your own city. Take notes, if you doubt your powers of recall! You should want to know what kind of housing the bird was kept in: Cages?—what size? Open wire, or closed, solid-sided box cages? Flights?—how big? What kinds of nests were used?—birds raised in wooden box nests, for example, will generally choose box nests when they reach breeding age. What kinds of utensils were used to provide seed and water? I've had Society Finches die of thirst because they were given open bowls of water, so I moved them into cages with tube-type waterers sticking through the wire instead. The more you reproduce the conditions the birds were used to, the better you'll do.

As you question the breeder from whom you're buying your stock, you may hear of his or her conviction that the birds are seasonal breeders. Usually you'll be told they breed only from late fall to early spring. Don't believe it. Goulds and the other well-domesticated Australian finches will breed at any time of year. Don't argue with the breeder; just give your birds a chance. If the breeder has been manipulating them, by varying day length and diet, for example, they may initially be on the same seasonal cycle being advocated by the breeder. Away from those controls, however, they'll go to nest whenever they are healthy and their other needs are met.

A pair of Gouldians can breed in a cage at least 18 in. cubed, but twice that amount of space is to be preferred. They will breed in colonies fairly successfully if housed in accommodations large enough so that nests don't have to be placed too closely together. They like to build nests from dried grass. Egg food helps bring them into breeding condition and gives them a convenient food to feed their babies.

Goulds show that they are in breeding condition by the colors of their beaks. Males get a bright red tip, or bright yellow tip in the case of yellow-heads, when they are in breeding condition, which is much of the time for males. Hens' beaks turn darker and darker as they come into condition, until in the middle of the breeding season their once-bone-white beaks may be jet black.

Goulds can breed when they're six months old, or even younger. There are records of pairs still in their juvenile plumage breeding when four months old. I set mine up to breed if they are six months old or older and if they have completed their first molt and are in full color.

Chestnut-breasted Mannikin (*Lonchura castaneothorax*). Once extremely rare, these interesting finches were imported in small numbers beginning in the late seventies. Dealers rarely have the opportunity to sex birds unless the sexual differences are obvious; in Chestnut-breasted Mannikins they're not, so customers were as likely to get mismatched pairs as they were to get true pairs. This contributed to the species's getting the reputation of being difficult to breed.

We started out with six birds, the least we ever try to start with when working with a new species. Once they were acclimated to their new environment, breeding quickly followed. Kept in a 35 sq. ft. *L*-shaped aviary, all three pairs proved to be correctly sexed and went to nest. They built voluminous nests in tin cans, wooden boxes, and wicker nests, and showed a preference for white feathers among the nesting

Top: The seeds of wild-growing grasses will also be accepted by finches. **Bottom:** Society Finch (Bengalese Finch, *Lonchura striata*).

materials offered. Clutch size averaged about five eggs.

Chestnut-breasted Mannikins are closely related to Society Finches and the other nuns and mannikins, and will hybridize with them. Young are uniformly brown. Only after they complete their first molt will they have the distinctive pattern of the adults. Six month-old specimens in our collection bred successfully, and, like many of the other Australian finches we've kept, they weathered occasional nights of temperatures in the twenties with no ill effects, even when they were breeding.

Their most distinctive characteristic is the song of the male. It's a repetitive, loud but monotonous pealing note. Its effect on most people who hear it is to inspire wonder at how such a small bird can have a song that persists so long without interruption for a breath.

Crimson Finch (*Neochmia phaeton*). The Crimson Finch is easily sexed, once it has gone through its first molt, because males show far more extensive red than hens. They like, but don't need, live food. There are three subspecies: black-, white-, and buff-bellied. The last is from New Guinea, so it's still possible to get wild- caught imports of that form. If so, pay special attention to their needs for privacy, live food, and room. Mine built a rather impressive dome-shaped nest on top of an open wicker canary nest, and lined it with oak leaves and fine fibers and feathers. They nested indoors, in a cage. I wired an oak branch to the side of the cage to give them greater privacy.

This species is reported to be aggressive, even dangerous, to other birds. I can't verify that. But because they're so scarce, I'd put the breeding imperative ahead of any desire to mix them with other species in a mixed collection.

Painted Finch (*Emblema picta*). This is one of the species I've never kept, but I'm looking forward to doing so. Happily, although it is still quite rare in the U.S., it is now being bred after an absence of more than a decade. The breeders I know, who are working with the species, are having mixed results; this will undoubtedly improve as more U.S.-bred specimens become available. The first few generations are always the toughest, and it is to the breeders

of them that we owe the greatest thanks. Management should be the same as for the other species described, although in an aviary you may want to try placing several nests near the ground; Painted Finches may find this particularly appealing.

Other Australian Finches. The Red-Browed Finch (*Aegintha temporalis*) is seldom if at all available in this country, though it is now being bred overseas and will eventually find its way here in significant numbers. Pictorella Finches (*Lonchura pectoralis*), relatives of the Society Finch, Chestnut-breasted Mannikin, and other mannikins and nuns, are now being bred in small numbers in the U.S. I doubt that they or their other Australian cousin, the Yellow- rumped Finch (*Lonchura flaviprymna*), will generate much excitement because they're relatively plain-colored birds.

The arrival of any species new to the U.S. is important, however, because someday our borders could be closed to importation. If this happens—it's happened before and has been threatened again and again—any species not in the country may never again become available to U.S. hobbyists. If our borders

had remained shut down after they were temporarily closed early in the seventies, Goulds, Shafttails, and Star Finches would be much scarcer than they are today. Others, such as the Crimson, Painted, and White-Breasted Gouldian finches, might not be here today at all.

There is little we, as conservationists, can do to protect the birds in their native lands, other than to report any activity we believe involves smuggled, wild-caught specimens. There is much we can do, however, to protect their future in the U.S. by applying all of our intelligence and resources to establishing them as free-breeders here. This challenge provides much of the excitement of aviculture today, and rightly so.

African Finches.

If the Australian finches are the most domesticated finches available to American fanciers, the African finches are the most readily available. They are trapped by tens of thousands in some African nations—they are protected in others—and

Species

imported into the U.S. after being quarantined in American holding stations. Sometimes they are also first quarantined in stations abroad.

Species that once were common to aviculture sometimes suddenly become scarce when governments change and the export of animal life is prohibited. Other governments relax their laws, permitting trapping to resume; then species that were rare arrive in the U.S. bird market in significant numbers.

Among the rarest and most desired are the Violet-eared Waxbill and the Purple Grenadier, two closely related birds, and Peters's Twinspot. All three species, because of their beauty, are highly sought after. They're imported just often enough, and in numbers just small enough, that breeders are familiar with them and prices remain high. But there are other African finches that are far rarer, or not available at all in the U.S., which, because they are not as spectacularly colored or because breeders here are not familiar with them, would generate little interest even if they did become available. The importation in

recent years of the Crimson Seedcracker, on the other hand, acquainted aviculturists with a seldom- seen species of dramatic beauty. The demand for them has exceeded the supply, so the price has been very high.

One of the advantages of high prices (it may be hard to imagine that there is any advantage!) is the economic incentive mentioned earlier. Because the prices are high, breeders will work diligently to master the mysteries of reproduction of Violet-eared Waxbills, Purple Grenadiers, and Crimson Seedcrackers. The task is not an easy one, since the supply of birds is extremely limited, but with time it is to be hoped we will establish easily-bred populations of these species and others. By virtue of the sheer numbers imported, others of the more common African finches will be bred, but there is no question less effort will be spent, on average, on these birds.

I've always believed that if importations of finches into the U.S. were to be cut off tomorrow, some of the birds we now characterize as the most readily available might quickly become the scarcest because we have not

77

Gold-breasted Waxbill
(Amandava subflava).

expended the efforts necessary to establish free-breeding populations of them. Quite simply, it has been too easy to go out and spend $10 or $20 to buy a replacement. Among these common species are the Cordonbleu, Fire-Finch, Strawberry Finch, Gold-breasted, Red-eared, and Orange-cheeked waxbills, and most of the nuns and mannikins. They may not always be available for as little as $20 each, but they are always less expensive than some of the rarer varieties mentioned, which sometimes sell for $100 per bird, and more. Whydahs and weavers are also frequently imported. Though not extremely expensive, they are rarely bred, but there are added reasons why this is the case with these birds.

I hope my point is not overlooked: even the commonest of the African, and Asian, finches—and in some ways, especially the commonest ones— have not been mastered by American finch breeders. They ought to be, so that if government regulations— ours or others'—change in coming years, these species will remain available to us from American- bred stock rather than via importation.

As discussed elsewhere, success with some of these species will hinge upon recognizing that they are wild-caught and conditioned environmentally to entirely different circumstances than the Australian finches, which are almost always captive-bred. Reacting to this circumstance properly may mean providing aviaries rather than cages; providing shrubbery or hiding places, so the birds feel secure, even if they are kept in a cage; feeding a variety of live foods; disturbing these birds far less than one would domesticated ones; and trying a wide range of other "tricks." You might try spraying them with a water mister, to simulate the rainy season. You can vary their diet and the length of time lights are left on each day, to bring them into breeding condition. Your own imagination is the guide.

Except as noted below, the African finches are peaceful and good prospects for a mixed aviary collection. Within a generation or two of captive breeding, with patience and intelligence, you may succeed in getting even wild-caught specimens to breed in relatively small cages. Once they

are acclimated, they need only a diet of good finch mix and clean water to survive. Diet supplements including either live food or egg food, which is an acceptable (and much more convenient) substitute, will keep them strong and healthy. These supplements are almost certainly necessary for breeding.

Most waxbills are small and extremely active birds. Some are easily sexed, while others are difficult. Many of them are very colorful. A collection including Cordonbleus, Fires, and Goldbreasted waxbills would display most of the colors of any artist's palette. Once acclimated, they are reasonably hardy.

Cordonbleu (*Uraeginthus bengalus*). Cordonbleus are the size of Zebra Finches. Blue extends from the face to the breast, flanks, and tail. The male is distinguished from the female by a red patch on each cheek.

Like other waxbills, Cordonbleus will nest in closed wicker nests. White or light-colored nesting materials seem to attract their attention and may stimulate nest building: try small white feathers and downy white yarn, strips of white tissue paper, and the like. Because these birds

are so often wild-trapped specimens, they are likely to want live food and to be stimulated into breeding when it is offered. Mealworms are the most common live food and the easiest to provide.

As is the case with almost all of the other waxbills, babies grow rapidly and leave the nest much sooner than Australian finches do—as early as two weeks of age, sometimes, compared to three to three-and-a-half weeks of age for the Australians. Young waxbills may not be self-feeding until they are five weeks old or older, so this is a dangerous period for them. Sometimes parent birds will begin another nest and stop feeding the young before they are old enough to feed themselves. If you are cage breeding, removing the nest can prevent this from happening. In an aviary, it is much harder to control this variable—like so many other variables—but it would be advisable, at least, to hang branches on the wall of the aviary opposite the nest. This way, if the babies fly out before they can completely control their flight, the chances of their injuring themselves by crashing into the far wall is minimized.

Blue-breasted Cordonbleu (*Uraeginthus angolensis*). This species is like the previous one, but the males lack the red cheek patch. Hens are duller than males, the blue covers less of their bodies. It will be difficult to distinguish hens of this species from hens of the previous one.

Blue-capped Cordonbleu (*Uraeginthus cyanocephala*). The Blue-cap bears the same, pretty blue plumage as the previous species, but the blue is more extensive, covering the entire crown of the male's head. The red cheek patch is absent. Hens can be distinguished from hens of the two previous species by their more lightly colored beak: it is red, whereas in the other two species it is reddish-gray with a black tip.

Violet-eared Waxbill (*Uraeginthus granatina*). The Violet-eared Waxbill, one of the larger waxbills, is a pretty finch. Males have a chestnut- red body and a purple face. Females are duller and easily distinguished from the males. Young birds of both sexes look like hens until they begin their first molt.

Juanita McLain and Dan and Carol Martin, members of our local bird club on Florida's west coast, have bred these birds in cages by fostering their eggs to Society Finches. Here at Bird Bay we got pairs in outdoor aviaries to lay, and then raised the young under Society Finches in cages indoors.

Our experiences with the Violet-eared Waxbill are a good example of the ways in which wild-caught birds can be more strongly influenced by their environment than domesticated birds. Despite our best efforts, we couldn't get ours to lay, until we began feeding termite larvae collected by Mike Hudson, a young aviculturist from a nearby city. The first pair began laying less than a week after we fed them termites. While it's hardly acceptable empirical data on which to base any conclusions, it's worth noting that when we removed the eggs for fostering, the birds did not go back to nest quickly, as is almost always the case with more domesticated birds. So we had Mike round up another batch of termite larvae and fed them on consecutive days to the Violet-ears. Again, within a week, the hen began to lay. This worked a third time, under similar circumstances, convincing me that at least with some pairs,

Cutthroat Finch *(Amadina fasciata)*.

termite larvae can be a powerful stimulus to breeding. I don't believe it was the protein content that stimulated the birds to breed so much as it was the possible psychological impact of consuming a food the birds had experienced in the wild. We had offered mealworms on previous occasions, and the birds ate them but did not go to nest. Obviously, experimentation can be very useful and should be tried with whatever African finches you may have in house at the time.

For the sake of your house, incidentally, you might not want to feed the termite larvae live, as we did, since some are almost certainly scattered about, to the potential peril of your home. Freeze the termites; immobilized, they may be slightly less appealing to the birds, but certainly more appealing to you and your neighbors.

Purple Grenadier *(Uraeginthus ianthinogaster)*. These close relatives of the Violet-eared Waxbill are easily sexed: the male has a brilliant purple-blue chest. They're stockier than Violet-eared Waxbills but otherwise very similar. Ours have proven hardy. Society Finches can raise the

young without great difficulty, and some of our friends succeeded in raising these birds in considerable numbers. They did not succeed, however, in establishing subsequent generations of captive-breeding populations from those young.

Melba Finch *(Pytilia melba)*. The Melba Finch is an extremely handsome, easily sexed, colorful African finch. In Australia this bird has been well domesticated since the government shut its borders to imports in the early sixties. If you can get specimens from Australia (the government there does permit exports of birds not native to Australia), your chances of breeding success will be greatly enhanced.

Male Melba Finches differ greatly in the intensity and extent of their coloration. Like so many of the other African finches, they prefer soft and light-colored nesting materials to dried grass. Because of their close ties to the wild, some Melbas and other waxbills are often more inclined to build complete dome-shaped nests of their own instead of using prefabricated wicker nests.

Peters's Twinspot *(Hypargos niveoguttatus)*. Peters's Twinspots are, in my opinion, one of the

handsomest finches available to aviculturists. Males have rich, red breasts and faces; hens are a softer chestnut color. Both sexes have bold, white dots on their flanks, on a black background. These are large birds, as large as any of the finches discussed in this book; canary-sized is the best way to describe them, perhaps. Their size has not prevented California breeders from breeding them in cages, nor did it prevent our Society Finches from raising full broods of up to four young, any of which were far larger than the Society Finches.

Our first pair that bred were housed in an outdoor aviary only 3 ft. wide by 6 ft. high by 7 ft. long, attached at one side to our house. A safety walk was at the far side. Several nests were placed up high on the wall of the house. A shelf projected from that wall, four feet from the ground, and two other nests (one box, one wicker) were mounted beneath the shelf. A juniper tree was planted in the middle of the flight, with a wicker nest fastened in it about four feet from the ground.

One day I couldn't find the hen. I checked all the nests without success. I then looked to the ground, expecting to find her dead. Suddenly, the frightened hen darted from beneath my feet. She had built a dome-shaped nest in a slight concavity in the ground, from which the top of the nest projected only slightly. Covered as it was with the same dried grass that littered the ground, it was virtually invisible. Inside the nest were four white eggs, which proved to be fertile. We fostered them to a pair of our Society Finches, which raised all four.

This experience was one more reminder of the importance of offering birds a variety of nesting sites. We've had parrot-finches and Owl Finches build their nests in the hollow part of concrete building blocks resting on the ground in their aviaries, even though a variety of seemingly more suitable nest sites were available. Put nests high, low, and in between. Use wicker and box nests. Try tin cans. Put every conceivable kind of safe nesting material in the cage or aviary. Mount the nests so they face different directions. Cover a corner of the cage or aviary to darken it. Experiment!

Green Twinspot (*Mandingoa nitidula*). Slightly smaller than

Peters's Twinspots and not as easily sexed, Green Twinspots are also very attractive, bearing as they do the breast and flank spots characteristic of the twinspots. They should prove capable of breeding for you. I know California aviculturists who have bred this species in small cages, and ours laid in aviaries comparable to the one described above. Males have a reddish orange "mask"; on hens, the mask is duller, more orange than red. Both sexes have interesting two-toned beaks, the black contrasting sharply with a bright waxy red.

Red-billed Fire-Finch (*Lagonosticta senegala*). While there are several different species of fire-finches that are occasionally imported from Africa, only one is common: the Red-billed Fire-Finch. The others vary in size and bill color, in the degree of red on the males, and in the color of the abdomen. Male Red-billed Fire-Finches are a rosy red above and reddish brown beneath. Hens are plainer, mostly reddish brown throughout. These small finches can be excellent breeders, though most efforts are plagued with failure because the parents do not find the food they instinctively (if not physiologically) need to feed their young.

I once imported fewer than half a dozen pairs of this species from Australia, where they had been cage-and-aviary-bred for more than ten years. They were domesticated, quite different from the usual wild-caught stock. I set three pairs up for breeding in relatively small cages, and within a month all three were on eggs. I removed the eggs from two pairs and fostered them under Society Finches. I left the eggs with the third pair, and they successfully raised two of three youngsters that hatched. This success, since I was not feeding live food, would almost certainly not be duplicated with wild-caught birds. The young are drab, like hens, but quickly begin to show red feathers if they are males, sometimes before they are old enough to be self-feeding.

Orange-cheeked Waxbill (*Estrilda melpoda*). This pretty bird can be an excellent breeder under the right circumstances, but is by no means established in American aviaries. You'll have to sex these birds by the comparison method outlined for the previous species: hens are duller.

Species

These munias are classified as a subspecies of the Chestnut Munia *(Lonchura malacca)*.

Gold-breasted Waxbill (*Amandava subflava*). The Gold-breast is one of the smallest finches, but it is reasonably hardy. There are records of specimens living eight to nine years in captivity. Hens are duller. If your Gold-breasted Waxbills won't go to nest, even if you've tempted them with white nesting materials, try bunching several fistfuls of hay into a tight bundle and wrapping it in chicken wire. Take a stick and poke small passageways into the interior of the hay ball, then hang it in your aviary. Gold-breasts, like many other waxbills, may find this an inviting environment and the necessary stimulus for breeding.

Other Waxbills. Lavender Waxbills (*Estrilda caerulescens*), Yellow-bellied Waxbills (*Estrilda melanotis*), and Red-eared Waxbills (*Estrilda troglodytes*) are frequently imported. Each species has its own characteristic appearance, and all are difficult to sex. Once acclimated, they're reasonably hardy and have bred in cages and aviaries.

Whydahs. Whydahs are a distinctive group of finches because the males have long, long tails. They have an eclipse plumage, in which they resemble nothing more than sparrows, concealing the true drama of their breeding plumage. They're also interesting because they are parasitic birds, laying their eggs in the nests of host species, which then raise the whydah young. As you might imagine, this compounds the difficulty of breeding these birds. They are generally peaceful enough to be included in mixed collections of finches and require no special diet.

Pintailed Whydah (*Vidua macroura*). The Pintailed Whydah is one of the more frequently imported whydahs. Naturally, you should exercise care in obtaining a pair, since the males resemble the females when they are out of color (in eclipse). Males in color are black and white, with bright red beaks and tails twice the length of their bodies. In the wild the hens lay their eggs in the nests of St. Helena and Red-eared waxbills. It would be reasonable to try to breed them in an aviary with pairs of those species, or, as an experiment, in a flight with Zebra Finches. If you can get a pair to go to nest in the absence of their usual host species, it is

– Diseases

highly likely Society Finches would raise the young.

Queen Whydah *(Vidua regia)*. Male Queen Whydahs are handsome black and brown birds with long tail feathers, two thirds of which are the bare shaft; only at the end are tufts of feathers found. The host species of this whydah is probably the Violet-eared Waxbill, making conventional breeding even more of a challenge: most breeders would be satisfied enough to get the Violet-ears to breed!

Paradise Whydah *(Vidua paradisaea)*. Perhaps the showiest whydah is the Paradise Whydah. It is larger than the previous species, and just as dramatic. Males out of color may be more richly marked than females, permitting sexing with greater accuracy than with some of the others.

If you've selected your birds properly, then the illnesses and injuries you must deal with will be ones acquired, contracted, or suffered while the birds are in *your* care. Think about this for a minute. Bird books characteristically contain a lengthy section on avian medicine, one that deals with medications and terminology more sophisticated than we expect to find in medical literature for ourselves or our children. Few among us can diagnose diseases with confidence, much less identify the treatment of choice.

For example: we *may* evaluate symptoms accurately enough to identify an intestinal infection or a respiratory ailment, but that still leaves us far short of the necessary information. A veterinarian would run two tests: one would identify the kind of bacteria causing the infection, if that is the case, to determine which antibiotics may be useful. A second test would determine the sensitivity of the unwanted intruders to a number of those antibiotics. Then, and only then, would treatment proceed, with the knowledge that we know what we're treating and what will treat it successfully. There's no comparison between

Diseases

this kind of attention and procedure and what you can learn from this or any other chapter in a book. If you haven't already sensed it, here's my advice for *treating* infectious diseases in your birds: find a good avian vet and use him or her.

Prevention.

The more important advice you can get here is how to keep your birds free of infectious diseases. First, follow the procedures outlined earlier for isolating your birds when they're first acquired and for acclimating them so that they aren't stressed when introduced to your collection. Next, make sure you feed them clean seed, keep their cages or aviaries reasonably clean, and—this is probably most important—keep their water clean. Don't underestimate the value of a varied diet too. Certain seeds may need to be in front of the birds at all times, but you can offer others periodically as treats. You can feed shredded carrots, spinach, dandelions, apple slices, and other dietary supplements rather than always offering a single green.

Finally, don't pamper them.

Help them become strong. You can do this in an aviary by keeping food on the floor, so they must fly up and down rather than merely hopping to conveniently located feeders. You can strengthen them by allowing them to experience varied temperatures too. You're not doing them a favor by keeping them at a constant, artifically maintained temperature. Your first worry should be how they will survive if you sell or trade them to others who do not provide such a benign environment. Even if that's not in your plans, what if there is a power outage and your bird room loses heat?

I remember a breeder in the Pacific Northwest who had a few Blue-backed Gouldian Finches. For two years I called him every few months to inquire about his progress with them. His collection was growing slowly—toward the day I was waiting for, when I could obtain some breeding stock from him. Then, on a winter night while he was away from home, a storm knocked out the electricity. All his Goulds, he lamented to me the next time we talked, had died that night. Interestingly, the temperature in his bird room had dropped only to about freezing. But that was more than 30 F. lower than the temperature they'd been kept at all their lives. That same winter my own Goulds, though in Florida, experienced the same temperatures. They were used to wild temperature fluctuations, so the winter freezes posed no problem for them.

I know veterinarians are expensive. And it's human nature to wonder whether it's necessary to make that costly trip. Finches do sometimes look terribly ill, then "snap out of it," for reasons we never entirely understand, within a day or two. The thing to remember is that an even greater number of them die shortly after they begin looking ill.

First Aid.

If you can't or won't get a bird to a good vet, there are a few stopgap measures you can take, and they can be life saving. Immediately remove the affected bird from whatever enclosure it is in and put it into a small, clean cage by itself. Make all the food items the bird is accustomed to available, unless the problem seems to be intestinal, in which

case it's probably best to offer only seed and water. Cover the cage on all sides but one. You can use a towel, cardboard, pillowcase, whatever. It's the function that matters: the cover will hold heat in and keep distractions out. The heat comes from a small, 25- or 40-watt light bulb which you should position at the only open side of the cage, at the end of a perch. The bird will regulate its temperature by moving closer to or farther away from the light. Remember too that if the bird is seriously ill, it may be too weak to mount a perch. If it's only barely able to stand on the floor of the cage, keep seed and water where the bird can reach it.

Sometimes in an emergency you'll want to treat the bird before you can get it to the vet's. For intestinal problems, try the same over-the-counter medications you'd use on yourself.

You've heard it before, and here it is again: prevention is much easier than treatment after the fact. There are numerous things you can do to prevent injuries, and all of them are easier than trying to treat an injury once it's occurred.

Trim your birds' claws so they don't get caught in nests or cage

wires. Birds rip their claws out this way and bleed to death; they get hung up and break a leg, or are found hanging, dead, from whatever snared them.

When you inspect your birds' homes, try to be paranoid for a moment; seek every potential peril. Wires once used to hold cuttlebone to the cage become potential snares; broken cage wires can hook a bird's band; cage wires spread slightly too far apart can allow a frightened bird to plunge its head through, but not get out again; some cage waterers work better as death traps than as sources of drinking water.

Even after you've identified and righted all of these perils, something else you can't anticipate will injure a bird. When that happens, while there's a great deal you can't do, there are a few simple things you can. Keep a styptic pencil with your bird supplies, to treat minor bleeding. If you don't have one, dust the injury with flour to coagulate the blood. Broken wings or legs can be restrained and held in place with tape and a toothpick splint. But if any of this seems simple, you're wrong. You'll soon see why vets are the option of choice. When you can't get to a vet,

however, leg injuries will sometimes heal best if the bird is isolated. It will stand on its one good leg, rest the other, and its recuperative powers can be remarkable. If you leave it with others, and it has to compete for a place at the feeder and dodge the advances of other birds, it may never heal.

If a feather breaks, remove the remainder by pulling the shaft straight out. If feet become scaly, use one of the commercially marketed preparations or apply petroleum jelly. The first application will seal and soften the scales; subsequent applications will lift the scales off as you rub the jelly in.

Summary: (1) Preventive measures are the best cure. (2) A good vet can do far more good than you can. (3) When you take treatment into your own hands, (*a*) isolate (*b*) heat and (*c*) treat.

Suggested Reading

ENCYCLOPEDIA OF SOFTBILLED BIRDS
By Dr. Matthew M. Vriends
ISBN 0-87666-891-0
TFH H-1026

Contents: Housing. Buying Birds. Feeding. Pekin Robins. Laughing Thrushes. Flycatchers. Thrushes. American Blackbirds and Orioles. Tanagers. Bulbuls. Leafbirds and Mousebirds. Honeycreepers, Flowerpiercers and Flowerpeckers. Sunbirds, Honeyeaters and Hummingbirds. Starlings and Mynahs. Barbets. Magpies, Jays and Crows. Pittas. Turacos. Cocks-of-the-rock. Toucans. Titmice or Tumblers and Nuthatches. White Eyes. New World Warblers.
Audience: Neglected in the existing literature is a big group of colorful, interesting, potentially profitable birds: the fruit-eaters and insect-eaters generally known as softbills. This excellently detailed new book, heavily laced with good full-color photos that show the birds at their best, covers every important housing and maintenance requirement (with special attention paid to feeding arrangements) of 19 different softbill groups. Ages 13 and older.

FINCHES AND SOFT-BILLED BIRDS
By Henry Bates and Bob Busenbark
ISBN 0-87666-421-4
TFH H-908

Contents: General Information. Care and Management. Finches. Softbills. Other Avicultural Subjects.
Audience: The most complete book on seed-eating, soft-billed birds (as opposed to "hard-billed" or parrot-like birds). Every important cage bird is discussed and illustrated in color. No other book in any language has so many birds known in the pet-bird world.

INTRODUCTION TO FINCHES AND SOFTBILLS
By Hank Bates and Bob Busenbark
ISBN 0-87666-762-0
PS-648

Contents: Diet. Aviaries, Equipment and Breeding. Diseases and Ailments. Australian Finches and Parrot Finches. Mannikins. Waxbills. Whydahs and Weavers. Buntings. European Finches. Goldfinches, Siskins and Serins. Miscellaneous Finches. Introduction to Popular Softbills.
Audience: For those just starting out with finches as a hobby, this will guide you through the better selection of various finches and will instruct the reader in the proper care and diet to avoid many errors which are commonly made. Ages 13 years and older.

Index